100

ACTIVITIES
FOR PRESCHOOLERS

Here are 100 ideas for activities you can do with preschoolers in your classroom or at home. Some activities are best suited for two year olds; others will be enjoyed most by four or five year olds. As you do these activities with your children, relate each activity to God's love and all that He does for us.

100 ACTIVITIES FOR PRESCHOOLERS

Published by David C. Cook Publishing Co.
850 N. Grove Ave.
Elgin, IL 60120
Cable Address: DCCOOK

Edited by Dave and Neta Jackson
Design: Christopher Patchel and Dawn Lauck

Printed in the United States of America

ISBN: 1-55513-138-7

Contents

BIBLE STORY ACTIVITIES

1 Sheepfold

Use this activity when you have a Bible story about Jesus, our Good Shepherd, or young David or any other person who was a shepherd.

Help children make a sheepfold by making a fence of blocks. Leave an open doorway. Place cotton balls inside of the fence for sheep. Move the sheep outside the sheepfold to eat grass; put sheep inside the sheepfold to sleep.

Option: Make a sheepfold of chairs; let children be sheep.

2 God the Creator

Have preschoolers help you look through old magazines and find pictures of things that God made (plants, animals, people). Tear or cut out the pictures and glue them on pieces of paper or grocery sacks.

Lead children in thanking God for His creations. Have a child point to each picture and say, "Thank You, God, for . . ." (*name object in picture*).

3 God Made . . .

Help children remember some of God's creations by playing a simple version of "Simon Says." After naming one of the many things that God created, do an action with your child. You might say, "God made the fish" as you pretend to swim, and "God made the birds" as you pretend to fly. End your game by saying these words from Genesis 1:31: "Everything God made was very good."

4 What Did Adam Need?

Have children imitate you as you act out some of the things Adam needed. Ask: "Who made the things Adam needed?" Then tear out magazine and catalog pictures of things God gives us— homes, food, water, plants, friends. Paste the pictures on construction paper, punch a couple of holes on one side, and tie the pages together with yarn to make a book. Write on the cover, "God Gives Us What We Need."

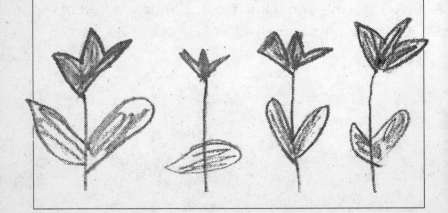

5 Animals in the Ark

Select an animal picture book and help children name animals Noah may have taken into the ark. Talk about how Noah obeyed God by building an ark and taking animals inside.

Children might want to gather stuffed animals. They could pretend to take the animals inside a boat made of chairs. Mention during the week that we obey God just as Noah did when we talk to God, do what Mom and Dad say, show love for others, etc.

6 Sharing Like Abraham

Your preschoolers will enjoy the story of Abraham and Lot if you provide some blocks to build a well and some cotton balls to represent sheep as in the first activity. Help crowd the cotton "sheep" all around the well, then divide them into two groups, as Abraham and Lot divided the land. Talk about how God wants families to get along. Encourage the beginning of sharing by giving children enough crayons or cookies so they can "share" some and still have plenty. At this point in their growth, just establish that sharing makes everyone happy.

7 God Gives Water

When preschoolers ask for drinks of water, talk about how God helped Moses and the people have water in the desert. Since we don't get water by hitting rocks, help child understand that the water from the faucet also comes from God. In a simple way describe how water from rivers and lakes comes into your house through pipes.

Then use some of that water to make lemonade or a fruit drink with a citrus fruit and sugar. As you add the water to your drink, tell children that many of the things we drink contain water.

8 King David's Throne Room

When presenting the story about Mephibosheth from II Samuel 9, use this roleplay activity to help children understand the significance of David's actions. This also is a helpful activity to introduce a discussion about disabilities. Help preschoolers understand that God made everyone special and He loves each person very much—that includes people with disabilities.

King David wanted to help his friend's family. Jonathan had a son who was lame. David sent Ziba (a man who used to work for Jonathan's family) to bring Mephibosheth, who couldn't walk like most people, to the palace so he could be kind to him.

To play-act this story, use three characters: King David; Ziba the servant; and lame Mephibosheth. To include more children, have people standing around to help King David or attendants to fan him.

Show children how to act when they play the part of Mephibosheth. Walk slowly, dragging one foot along. If some of the children start to giggle, encourage them to be kind.

Since this is a short scene, go through it several times, letting different children take the speaking parts. They will need help the first few times to know what to say.

9 Bringing the Offering

To help preschoolers learn about the importance of the offering, pretend that you are a Bible-time leader. You could drape a shawl or stole around your neck as the temple helpers did in Bible times. Announce the time for the people (children) to prepare for the offering by saying, "Come to the temple! Put your offering money in the offering box." Place a special container on a table. Use this container for this purpose each Sunday. You may want to act out a portion of the story about King Joash taking offerings to repair the temple (II Chron. 24:1-14) or a similar passage. Children can put coins in the container for the offering and give just as Joash and the people did.

10 Building the Wall

In advance, when telling the story of Nehemiah building the wall (see Nehemiah 2), prepare a section of wall or room divider so that it is blank. Give each child a sheet of construction paper in a color contrasting to the blank wall.

Have one child bring his paper and stand in front of the group. Say, "Here is a worker who wants to help build the wall. He has a building block." Have him take his building block and tape it on the wall just above the floor. Then say, "He has done his work and used his building block to build a wall. But his one building block didn't make a whole wall. He doesn't have any blocks left. How can we get a whole wall?" Other children will volunteer to use their building blocks.

Let children tape their blocks, one at a time (like laying bricks), to the wall, adding to those already there. Allow children to "lay" more than one brick, especially if your group is small. When the wall is completed, talk about what a good job was done because everyone worked together.

11 Working Together

Here is a variation of the above activity. Work together to build a wall of blocks or Legos just as Nehemiah and the people worked together to build a wall around the city of Jerusalem (see Nehemiah 2). Then act out ways people at your church work together—a choir practicing, a class cleaning up a Sunday school room, and so forth. Act out ways families work together such as raking leaves, cleaning up toys.

12 Happy Birthday, Jesus

Near Christmastime, print the words "Happy Birthday, Jesus" on a paper for your child to decorate with crayons. (*Idea: Put a line of glue along the letters; let child sprinkle with glitter.*) Help child hang the paper up as you sing "Happy Birthday" to Jesus several times.

13 Water from a Well

When telling a Bible story that refers to a well—Jacob meeting Rachel or the story of Jesus and the woman at the well—demonstrate for preschoolers what a well was like. Using toy figures and a large bowl of water, make a "well" by taping string to a small plastic cup and dipping it into the water. Let children take turns hauling water from the well. This simple activity will help them understand the story and what life was like in Bible times.

14 I'm Sorry

Use this simple activity to help children understand that Zacchaeus was sorry for his wrong actions. Draw a happy face on one side of a paper plate and a sad face on the other side. As you tell the story in Luke 19:1-10, have children show the side of the plate which matches how Zacchaeus felt. At the end of the story, talk about how happy Zacchaeus felt because Jesus cared for him. End this time by saying a prayer thanking God for loving us even when we do wrong things.

This same activity can be used for any story in which people felt sad and then happy—such as Peter's denial, how Jesus felt when Lazarus died, and so forth.

15 Being a Good Samaritan

Tell the story of the good Samaritan from Luke 10:25-37. Pause after telling about each character who saw the hurt man and ask, "Does Jesus want us to be like that person?" Children will imitate your actions as you shake your head and answer "yes" or "no." Let children practice putting plastic bandages on a doll just as the Samaritan helped the hurt man. Then help children think of ways to be good Samaritans at home by doing kind things.

16 Bartimaeus Can See!

After telling the story of blind Bartimaeus in Luke 18:35-43, have children use the side of a dark crayon to fill a piece of paper with a dark color. Explain that this is how everything looked to Bartimaeus when he was blind. Then reread the last part of the story. Help children think of things Bartimaeus saw when Jesus healed his eyes. Turn paper over and let children scribble color with bright colors like blue for the sky, yellow for the sun, and green for the grass.

17 Jesus Helps Us See

Help children understand more about blindness by playing a game. Show a familiar object such as food or a toy. Ask children to tell you what the object is. Then tell children to close their eyes. Can they see the object now? Can they remember what the object is? Have children open their eyes, and name the object again. (Repeat the game with another item.)

Remind children that Jesus made the blind man able to see by touching his eyes. Jesus cares about all the problems and joys in your child's life.

18 Jesus and the Fishermen

In a large basin with an inch or two of water (or at bath time at home), provide some toy boats or fish. You might have fun making boats from meat trays. As children play, talk about how Jesus met some fishermen and went out in a boat with them. If you have a colander, sieve, or a piece of netting to scoop up toys, children will better understand how the fishermen used nets to catch fish. How nice to know that Jesus wanted some fishermen to be His helpers. We can learn to be Jesus' helpers, too.

19 Friends Like Jesus

During the preschool years, children need time to develop social skills. A good way to practice is for children to "visit" each other. Help children prepare for a friend's visit just as Mary, Martha, and Lazarus prepared to have their friend Jesus come. Children can help fix a simple snack, lay out the plates and napkins, get out some toys. Talk about the importance of sharing things and how fun it is to get ready for a friend's visit.

20 Early Christians

Help preschoolers name the things the early Christians did when they met together. (See Acts 1, 2: They prayed and ate, sang and shared.) Point out that these are things which children today do at Sunday school. Older preschoolers may enjoy being leaders—they may want to take turns saying brief prayers or suggesting favorite songs. Provide a snack (fruit slices or crackers) that children can thank God for and share together.

You can do these things at home, too. Look for times to give thanks spontaneously with your child. When you enjoy something together, pause in your fun to thank God for all the good times and blessings He has given you. If your extended family or friends gather for a holiday feast, remember to celebrate the way the early Christians did.

21 Let's Catch Some Fish

Let preschoolers pretend they are Bible-time fishers. Since only nets were used back then to catch fish, this activity will challenge children to try to throw out their nets and haul in some fish the way people did in Jesus' day. Put blue fabric on the floor to represent the water. Then put paper or plastic fish on the water. Make fish nets from coarse fabric netting or from mesh bags in which grocers package potatoes and oranges. Weight the nets to make them easier to throw by taping pennies to the edges.

LEARNING ACTIVITIES

22 God's Rules Make Us Happy

Play a game that reinforces God's rules. Let each child draw a happy face on one side of a paper plate, and a sad face on the other side. Each time you name something God wants us to do, have the child show the happy face. If you name something God doesn't want us to do, have child show the sad face. As you play, explain in simple terms the reasons behind life's do's and don'ts.

23 Touch and Taste

Have foods with different textures, shapes, and taste such as fuzzy peaches, smooth apples, bumpy carrots, and skinny bananas.

Touch: To help children concentrate on touch, have them close their eyes and feel the fruit and other foods. Tell children to guess the names of the foods they are feeling.

Taste: Cut the fruits or vegetables into small slices and put them on napkins for children to taste. Also encourage them to use their sense of smell to guess what it is.

24 Do as I Do

Have children sit down on the floor around you with their eyes closed. Then make sounds as the children listen.

• Clap your hands, click your tongue, sing a song, etc. Then ask children to try to figure out how you made the sounds and to try to imitate you.

• Use objects to make different sounds. For example, bounce a ball and tap toys such as blocks together to make interesting sounds. Then have children open their eyes and point to what you used to make the sounds.

25 Shadows

Use a bright light to make shadows in the room. Have children look at their shadows. Are the shadows bigger or smaller than the children are? Can they make the shadows change? How? Notice shadows of other objects. Do they all fall on the same side?

Go outside. Look at shadows of big things—a car or building. Stand on the shadow side, then on the sunny side. What difference do you feel?

26 Noise Hunt

God gave us ears for listening. Sit or stand quietly in one place outside and listen to noises. Encourage children to name noises they hear—birds, wind, etc. Try imitating the sounds. Then, if you wish, return inside and make a list of all the noises. Draw pictures of things that made noise.

27 Map

Cut out a construction paper church resembling your own church building. Place it in the center of a large sheet of paper or bulletin board. Also cut out a car from an ad or from construction paper. Ask the children on which side of the church building you should park the car. What else needs to go nearby to make this more like "our church"?

After a few questions have been raised, suggest going outside to check. Walk around the church building and let children point out what they should put on the map. Back in the room they may draw and cut out cars, trees, neighboring houses, and other items to complete the map. When the map is finished, thank God for your church. Pray for people in the neighborhood.

28 Rock-collecting Walk

Two good things about collecting rocks are: (a) There always seems to be enough for everyone; (b) the children don't spoil any gardeners' work. Just after a rain or at a pond's edge they will find pretty, wet rocks. Put them in jars of water. Other things to do with rocks are:

1. Place them on paper plates according to size, color, or another feature. Make a label for each plate: small rocks, shiny rocks, etc.
2. Paint eyes and other features to make pet rocks.
3. Lay the rocks in a row in order from small to large, dark to light. Count them.

29 Picture Hunt

In advance: Cut out pictures of things children enjoy from magazines, newspapers, or toy catalogs. Mount the pictures on construction paper so they will be sturdier. Try to find enough pictures so that there are at least two or three for each child. Hide these pictures around the room.

When children arrive, have them go on a "picture hunt." Each child should stop looking and sit down when he or she has found the limit of two or three pictures. (This will allow everyone to find some.)

Then have children sit in a circle. Ask each child to tell about his or her pictures with the group. Ask simple questions to stimulate conversation.

30 Weather Fun

Give each child four 4" x 4" sheets of paper. Help each child make diagonal marks on one for rain; dots on one for snow; a large circle with sunburst effect for the sun. On the last page put a copy of the following poem for parents to read to them. Fasten the sheets together at one corner with paper fastener. Children can turn from page to page as you repeat this poem:

Jesus helps me in the rain;
Jesus helps me in the snow;
Jesus helps me in the sunshine.
Jesus is my Friend, I know.

31 Nature Center

As spring approaches, begin a nature center. Use a table or low shelf where children can see and handle the things on display.

Potted plants and flowers in vases are appropriate—but don't limit yourself to garden flowers. Wild flowers and even dandelions can be beautiful. Encourage children to bring in things for the center. Treat any contribution as an important creation of God. Look especially for a discarded bird's nest, a branch of new leaves, pussywillows.

As summer approaches children might add shells from a vacation at the beach, little stones from other places they visit, and so on. Remind them not to take things from state and national parks, and not to hurt any growing plant.

Keep changing objects at your nature center to keep interest high. Use items to talk about God's plan for growing things, the seasons, etc.

32 Seasons Tree

Put four branches in a pot of sand. Divide children into four groups and assign each a branch to "dress" for a certain season. Use construction paper to make the following:

Spring: Small buds and blossoms.

Summer: Green leaves and butterflies.

Fall: Colored leaves with apples.

Winter: Snow (cotton) and maybe a cardinal.

33 Follow the Leader

Provide each child with a large sheet of construction paper which has been divided into equal fourths. Explain that you are the leader and they are the followers in this game.

Then draw a square, a circle, a rectangle, or a triangle in any of the four squares. The children must follow the leader by drawing the same shape in the same square on their own paper. If you color the shape, children should color their shape the same color. Repeat this three times, using a different shape in each square.

Or choose different children to be the leaders.

34 Let's Pretend

Ask children to take turns pretending to do different kinds of jobs people have. Have the rest of the children guess what the job is. If children have trouble thinking of jobs, suggest mail carrier, waiter, nurse, bus driver, baker, and pastor.

35 Miniature House

Provide small boxes such as shoeboxes so children can make a miniature home. Remove the lids and turn the boxes on their sides so they look like open rooms in a dollhouse. Let children choose which room in the house they would like to work on—living room, kitchen, bedroom, bathroom, garage, etc. Children can create miniature furnishings to glue in the boxes with materials such as nut cups, cardboard, spools, fabric, jar lids, small gift boxes (the size that jewelry comes in), and colored paper. When the rooms are done, stack and tape the boxes together to make a miniature house.

36 All Week Long

The disciples found comfort in knowing that Jesus would be with them even when they were separated. Children do not always understand what happens when people go away. Talk about people the children may see only once a week such as the pastor or Sunday school teacher. What do they think these people do during the week? Tell what you do. If you know, tell them what the pastor does during the week. Help them understand what a parent who works outside the home does.

37 On the Go

In advance: Cut pictures of transportation vehicles (cars, trucks, planes, trains, bicycles, etc.) from magazines and coloring books. Also cut out pictures of familiar objects that could not be used for transportation. Place all the pictures on the table. Have the pupils point to the transportation pictures and identify them. Encourage your preschoolers to tell you how those things are used.

38 Jesus Loves My Friends

Help child name all the children he or she knows. Print the names on a list and talk about how Jesus loves all these children.

39 Pet Shop

Play "pet shop." Use cardboard boxes for cages and stuffed animals for pets. Let children take a pretend trip to purchase a pet. Name the different stuffed animals and make their sounds as you look at them. Ask: "Would this animal make a good pet?" (Tigers and teddy bears would be happier in the forest.) As you look in each cage, ask, "Who made this animal?" And after you answer this question together, say, "And everything God made was good."

40 It's Important!

Name things that are important to you. Help children name things that are important to them such as sleeping with a favorite stuffed animal. Then have them cut out pictures from magazines of things that are important to Jesus. Then help them realize that everyone is important to Jesus, and He cares about what is important to us.

41 Making Figures

Make play dough or gingerbread figures. As you work together, say that God made our arms, legs, shoulders, and heads. Have child point to the body part mentioned. Then talk about the things each body part can do. Arms reach, eyes see, and so on.

42 What Does It Need?

As you look at books with children, play "What Does It Need?" Point to various people and animals and ask what each needs. Perhaps children will think of food, shelter, or a hug. This game will help them start the lifelong task of putting others first.

43 Love Gift

Give a child a surprise gift such as a lollipop, a special sticker, small pack of crayons, or even a hug—just because you love him or her. Explain when you give the gift or hug that God does the same thing for His children. He gives us good things just because He loves us.

44 Watch Them Grow!

In early spring, plant marigold seeds (or any hardy annual) in small pots on a window sill. Talk about how we need to water the plant, but God puts life into the seeds and makes them grow. Let children squirt a spray bottle to keep plants moist. If possible, plants seedlings outside when danger of frost is past.

45 What's This For?

Play "What's This For?" pointing to different parts of our bodies. Ask what each part does to help us: feet help us walk, fingers help us color pictures, and so on. Let child try brushing his or her hair without bending an arm to show how important the elbow is to the body. Say, "Isn't it wonderful how God made our bodies to work for us?"

46 Pretend Sunday School

Let children take turns pretending to be the teacher telling about God at Sunday school. Provide a few props: a small table for an altar, a child's Bible, and some Sunday school cards. The "pupils" might be a few dolls. The "teacher" can lead everyone in singing and tell a Bible story.

47 Sorting It Out

Help children learn to categorize by giving them buttons to sort by color. If children do not know the colors, let them sort by size. Explain that God helps us learn how to do things so that we can help one another.

48 Making a Puzzle Person

Have a child lie on a large sheet of wrapping paper. Draw an outline of the figure. Then have the same child or another child lie on another sheet of paper. Draw an outline of the figure. Cut out the second figure, then cut it into six pieces—the two arms, the two legs, the body, and the head. Let preschoolers use this as a jigsaw puzzle, putting the pieces in the proper place on top of the first outlined figure. As children play, talk about our bodies and how wonderfully God has made them.

49 Water and Fish

Give each child a blue crepe paper streamer two feet long and show how to move it gently, pretending to be water. Begin slowly and gradually have the children move their streamers faster and faster as if the water is moving quickly.

Collect the streamers and have children put their hands together and pretend to be fish. As they "swim" around the room, quietly say:

The fish are gently swimming, swimming, swimming.
The fish are gently swimming through the water.

Change the tempo of the words to let the children move faster or slower.

50 Feeding Time

Put a goldfish in a bowl and fish food on a table. Have children stand next to the table and watch the fish swim around. Explain that it is important to keep hands out of the bowl or the fish might be frightened.

Put a little fish food in the bowl and watch as the fish eats. Or if you have only a few children, give each child a flake of fish food and help them individually drop the food into the bowl.

Ask: "How does a fish move? What happens when food is dropped in the water?" Explain that God made fish to live and breathe in water. Everything God made is very good.

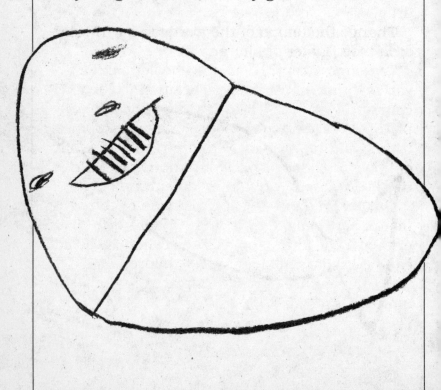

51 Our Community

Begin a community mural that you may want to keep up for several weeks. Find a wall, bulletin board, room divider, or window where you can begin arranging your community.

Buildings: Make a house pattern children can use, or let them draw their own houses to cut from construction paper. Include houses, stores, and apartment buildings. Preschoolers who are less advanced manually may prefer to have you do the cutting, especially around doors and windows. Let them color houses on white paper, draw bricks, and so on.

Trees and flowers: Add construction paper trees and flowers to the mural.

Transportation: Have preschoolers add a variety of methods of transportation to their community mural. They may draw (or cut out) pictures of cars, trucks, buses, taxis, airplanes, trains, and bicycles. Let children tell how many of these methods of transportation they have used. How many would they like to try?

Option: Roll up several 6" squares of construction paper to make cylinders. Children can paste or tape a car to the top of these cylinders, which can be used as holders so the children can "drive" their cars to different places in the community.

52 Thank-You Banner

Use the words "Thank You, God" to make a banner for the community mural or any other bulletin board that depicts things for which we should thank God. Project the words from an overhead projector onto a large sheet of paper and trace around them, color, and cut out. Paste the words to a bright ribbon or paper banner and add balloons made from paper circles and strings. Ask children to name friends in the community for whom they are thankful.

53 From Farm to Store

Let preschoolers make matching farm and store pictures. Show on one sheet of paper what a food item looks like as it comes from a farm; on another paper, show that same food in a supermarket. *Examples:*

    Cow with pail of milk by it; plastic jug of milk.
    Chicken by eggs in a nest; carton of eggs.
    Corn in a field; corn in a can.
    Apple tree; bag of apples.
    Pumpkin patch; pumpkin pie.

These pictures can be previously cut from magazines and pasted on construction paper. Connect the pictures with string or yarn. You might title this display "God Gives Us Good Things to Eat."

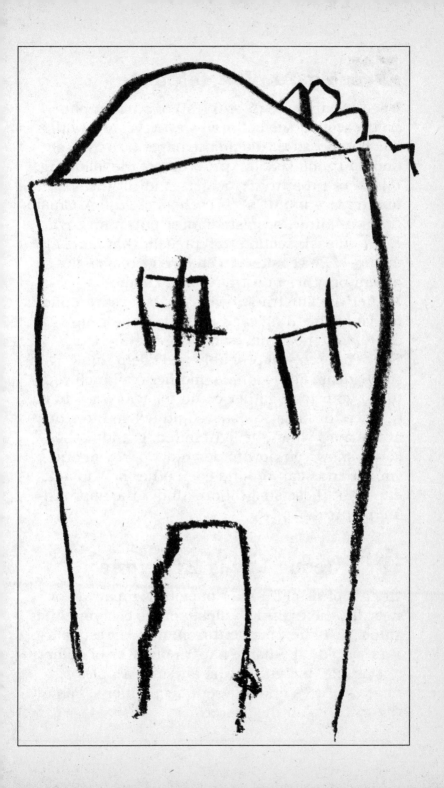

54 My Family Helps Me

Place a long piece (5 or 6 feet) of butcher paper on the wall at the children's eye level and with a crayon or marker divide the paper into five sections. In each section, print one of the following: "Mothers"; "Fathers"; "Sisters and Brothers"; "Grandparents"; "Us" (preschool children). Children can draw, or paste figures cut from magazines, in each section to represent that family member. Be sensitive to children from single-parent or other non-traditional families.

After the illustrations are up, have each child tell you something each of the various people could do to help him or her do what is right. Your children will probably need help thinking of some ideas. For example, mother could tell you to eat your food, father could tell you when to go to sleep, brother or sister could tell you to stop at the curb when the light is red, grandmother could show you how to do your work, you and your friends can remind each other how to act, etc. Print these suggestions under the appropriate pictures.

55 Jesus Loves Everyone

Hang a piece of butcher paper low on a wall or door. At the top print: "Jesus loves everyone the same." Children may cut from magazines, catalogs, or old take-home papers pictures of different people. Include young and old, people of different races and different occupations. Paste the pictures on the poster.

56 God Cares for His Creations

In advance, prepare a piece of shelf or butcher paper for a mural. Divide the mural into four sections. At the top of each section paste a picture of one of the following: a bird; an animal; a flower; a child. Below each picture children may paste things God gives His creations—berries, seeds, and twigs for the bird; perhaps pictures of grass and a pond for the animal; a sun and raindrops for the flower; pieces of dry cereal, cloth, and pictures of houses and families for the child.

57 Out on the Lake

Tape a length of butcher or shelf paper to the floor with masking tape. Draw a blue oval on the paper to represent a lake. Provide the children with crayons, scraps of construction paper, blunt-edged scissors, cotton balls, and paste or glue to make fluffy clouds, sun, boats, etc. Help children add these items to the picture, showing them how to make boats from triangles and rectangles.

Pretend that a storm starts on the lake. The wind is blowing (everybody blow). Change the picture to show that it is stormy. Help children draw big waves on the lake. Cut a dark cloud out of paper and paste it over the sun.

58 What Do I Do All Day?

Provide each child with a paper on which you have already drawn a sun. The sun should be in different positions on different papers—at the upper left for morning, at the top middle for noon, at the upper right for afternoon, and way over to the right as if setting at night. Help children decide what time of day each picture would be and what they would be doing at that time. Older preschoolers may want to draw a picture of getting dressed in the morning. Another child may want to draw himself or herself playing outside with friends in the middle of the day. Another child may wish to portray an evening scene such as getting ready for bed.

After children have drawn pictures, post them in order from morning until night on a bulletin board or mural. Talk about how God takes care of us throughout the entire day, no matter what happens.

59 Fill the Ark

Cut out a large ark from brown butcher paper and tape it to a wall. Let children color or cut out and paste on pairs of animals. Decorate the animals with scraps of yarn and fake fur.

60 God Made the Seasons

Cover a table with a long piece of butcher paper. Mark it off into four sections: summer, fall, winter, and spring. Label the mural with the words "God Made the Seasons."

Have the children scribble color in each of the different sections. Provide them with colors related to each of the seasons. For summer provide bright colors such as yellow and bright blue; for fall provide colors such as brown, gold, and maroon; for winter provide gray and white; spring colors might be green, lavender, and pink. Adjust color choices according to the seasons in your particular area.

Option: Provide collage materials for the children to paste onto the mural. For example, strips of foil can be spring rain; a yellow circle can be the summer sun; torn paper or real leaves can represent fall; and cotton can be winter snow.

CHARACTER-BUILDING ACTIVITIES

61 Building God's House

Secure a rather large cardboard carton. A stove carton would work very nicely; check with an appliance store to obtain one. Draw windows and cut out a door, so children may enter. Children can help paste on curtains made from facial tissues at the windows. Children may help you build pews of blocks. At the front of the church, make a small table of blocks and place a Bible on it. Ask children to suggest other things that might go in the church.

62 Telephone Line

Play "telephone" with the children. Have them sit in a circle while you whisper to the first child, "Jesus loves you." Then let that child whisper the message to the child next to him or her and so on around the circle. Have the last child say the message aloud. You might let your preschoolers think of other messages about Jesus they can send.

63 Playing Church

Let children act out going to church. Some children can be the congregation, the choir, and the ushers. Let children take turns being the minister.

Ask children to play other helpful things at church. They may act out ways they can help, such as sweeping the floors, setting up chairs, and so on.

64 Christmas All Year

When you take down your Christmas tree, keep one ornament in your room. Choose one which will remind children of the Christmas message that Jesus is the promised Savior—a star, an angel, or a tiny Nativity scene. Hang the ornament in a place where the children will see it often and remember that God sent Jesus to be our Savior at Christmas and all year long.

65 When I'm Scared

Have older preschoolers get together in pairs or small groups to act out some scary situations. (Suggestions: thunderstorm; barking dog; "monsters under the bed"; the dark; etc.) After each skit, let volunteers name and then act out ways to let God help. (They can pray, talk to their families so they can help; sing a song about God; and so on.)

66 We Can Worship

Talk about the various skills that God has given each child and how each preschooler can use his or her skills to share in God's work. Then help children plan a mini worship service so that youngsters can use their skills. Pick a theme for the service ahead of time so all of the children's efforts will emphasize the chosen theme. Let children choose what they'd like to do:

• Play rhythm instruments and/or sing a simple worship song.
• Work on a group prayer or action rhyme to recite together.
• Illustrate a favorite Bible story by drawing pictures, painting a mural, or making a sculpture.
• Act out the Bible story.
• Set up and arrange items such as chairs and art displays.

If the group is small, just one child might do each job, or the jobs could overlap. Just be certain that each child is given the opportunity to participate actively and to contribute to the group effort.

67 This Is the Way We . . .

Help children think of ways they might help a sick friend. Then let children pretend to do these things. For example, if someone suggests, "Take flowers," the following steps may be acted out: walking to the garden; picking the flowers; carrying them carefully to the sick friend's house; ringing the doorbell; greeting the friend's mother at the door; presenting the flowers to the mother to give to the friend; saying good-bye; skipping home.

68 Friends Help Each Other

God showed Elisha how to be a good friend to a woman and her sons. Pray with children that God will help all of you show friendship. Then help children plan friendly gestures you can do together for someone who needs help.

• Prepare food and deliver it to someone who is sick.
• Take an elderly person grocery shopping.
• Transport a neighbor child to Sunday school.
• Help rake a neighbor's lawn.

69 A Friend Loves

Do you know someone who is sick, shut-in, or just lonely? Sending cards to friends and involving preschoolers in mailing them will be meaningful. Encourage children to draw a special picture to include. Imagine the smile on someone's face when a card arrives saying, "A friend always loves you."

70 Weather-Wise

What weather is it today? Thank God for the weather—no matter what it is—during prayer time. Avoid labeling weather as "nice" or "bad." Instead, talk about how all kinds of weather help us and the animals and plants.

Show pictures of types of things such as boots, sunglasses, umbrellas, swimsuits, and wool scarves, that are needed for different weather conditions. Have children guess the type of weather during which each is used.

71 Sunlight Delight

Make a point to look with your child for sunshine, shadows, and clouds each day. We often take daylight for granted, especially in a city where the sky maybe crowded out by buildings. Tell children that God created the sun that shines as they work and play. Take a walk and point out things that people can do during the day. You may see someone mowing the grass, watering flowers, or riding a bicycle. Note that the bright sun gives us light even when it is behind a cloud.

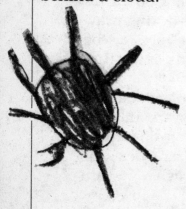

72 Signs of the Seasons

Weather permitting, take a nature walk with children to see signs of the season, whichever one it may be. If you take your walk during spring, point out to them the buds on trees, birds returning, warmer weather, and crocus blooming. Sing a song about that season while you walk.

73 Rain, Rain, It's Okay

When it rains, remind children of the story of Noah and the ark. Forty days was a long rain! If the rain is not too hard, dress appropriately and take a walk outside. Thank God for the beautiful trees, animals, grass, and flowers that are getting a bath and a drink. Be ready to look for rainbows when the sun shines during a summer shower. Talk about how we obey God when we thank Him as Noah did.

74 Sharing God's Love

Share God's love. This activity can be done in the classroom or at home. Make mini-hearts from red scrap paper. Hide a few around the room, under things or in pockets. Tell the finder of each heart, "I love you and so does God."

Share love and cheer others. Draw simple hearts on postcards and let children color them. Add a message of God's love and send cards to neighbors and your pastor.

75 Naughty Dolls

Have children pretend dolls or stuffed animals are doing wrong things, such as running in the room, or pushing someone. Help children talk to their dolls about the wrong things they are doing. Encourage children to hug and show love to their dolls even though they have done wrong things.

76 Sharing Cookies

Bake a favorite sugar cookie recipe with the children. Write special messages on little slips of paper, roll them up, then shape some dough around each little roll of paper and bake. Be sure to explain the messages to the preschoolers since they can't read. Have them help you think of people to whom they can give the cookies—church neighbors, shut-ins, a friend who's been sick. Messages can fit various holidays:

Christmas: "Hallelujah! Jesus is born."
Valentine: "Jesus loves you; I do, too."
Thanksgiving: "We thank God for you."

77 Playing Animals

Here are some ways preschoolers will enjoy pretending to be animals:

• Suggest that some children pretend to be pets, such as cats and dogs. Other children can take care of them by "feeding" them and taking them for a walk.

• Pretend to have a zoo. Make block enclosures and let some children be the animals in the zoo. Others may be the zoo keepers and take care of the animals.

• Children might enjoy having a parade in which each pretends to be a certain animal. Make animal noises as you walk around the room.

78 Penny Walk

On a nice day, go for a penny walk. Walk to the corner and flip a penny. Heads you go one way, tails you go another way. Where will you end up?

79 Noise Makers

For each child, place a few beans or buttons in a small plastic container or ice-cream carton (pint size). Tape the lid securely to the carton. Children will delight in shaking this rhythm instrument and marching in time with music. Let the children suggest happy songs to sing while they shake their instruments.

80 'Holes' to Crawl Through

To help get out the wiggles, let preschoolers crawl through "holes." These holes could be under tables or adult-size chairs, through large boxes; or the holes could be created when you stand with your legs apart or lean against the wall.

81 Mother, May I?

Play the traditional game, "Mother, May I?" Explain to children that you are the leader, and in this game the leader is called "Mother." Place children side by side in a line. Stand about three yards in front of them and, speaking to one child at a time by name, give an order—take three little steps, or two giant steps, or two big hops, and so on. Vary your orders, but be sure the children are able to do what you are asking. Some preschoolers have trouble jumping, skipping, or hopping on one foot.

Instruct children that the rules of the game say that they must remember to ask, "Mother, may I?" before they do what was commanded. Answer the child by saying, "Yes, you may!" If a child forgets to ask permission first, he or she loses a turn.

Be sure to give each child several opportunities to move forward. The winner is the first child to reach the area where you are standing.

82 Sandals

Draw a pattern around the child's stocking feet on poster board or cardboard. Make the pattern a little larger than the child's feet. Lace yarn or strips of fabric through holes at the toes and the heels. Tie the yarn or fabric at the ankle and over the toes.

83 Free-Form Collage

Have ready a large piece of shelf or butcher
paper and a variety of collage materials such as:
scraps of fabric; tissue paper; yarn; macaroni; or
buttons. Explain that a collage is a picture made
from all different kinds of materials. Give each
child all of one type of material. If you do not
have enough variety of materials, give two or
three children all the yarn and another pair all
the buttons, etc.

Let children glue their items onto the shelf
paper in any way they wish. As they work, talk
to them about working together.

84 Bean Bag Toss

Make a bean bag toss game. Bean bags can be made of two 6" squares of fabric filled with rice or beans and stitched securely together.

To make a target, tape four shoe boxes together: (1) tape two boxes side by side; (2) tape a third box across the top ends of the first two boxes; (3) tape the fourth box across the bottom ends.

Number the boxes 1 through 4. The box at the bottom should be number 1, the two boxes in the middle should be 2 and 3, and the box at the top should be 4.

Children can take turns throwing bean bags, trying to toss the bags into the number 4 section. Talk about how much fun it is to play together as well as to work together.

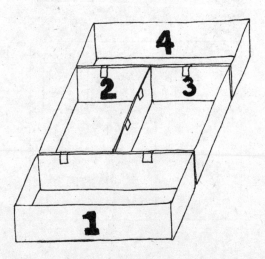

85 House Puzzle

Give each child the following construction paper shapes: 4" square, two 1" squares, a 1" x 3" rectangle, and a triangle measuring 5" across the bottom and 3 1/2" on either side. Children will also need an 8 1/2" x 11" piece of construction paper. Have them paste or glue the shapes on the construction paper to make a house. Rather than making a sample for the children to copy, you might help them think through what shapes would go where to make a house.

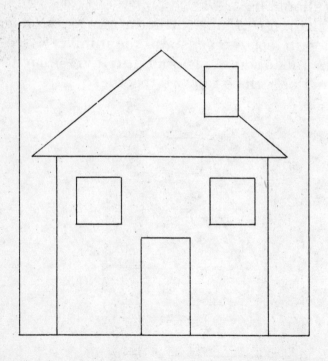

86 Airplane on a String

Cut a simple airplane shape from a piece of cardboard or heavy paper. Punch a hole in the top of the plane. Tie one end of a 10-foot piece of string to a chair or another piece of furniture. Thread the loose end of the string through a hole in the plane. Push the plane all the way back to the chair. Stretch the line of string out straight and give the end to a child to hold.

Let each child take a turn jiggling the string carefully to get the plane to move toward him or her.

FAMILY ACTIVITIES

Use these ideas with your own family or send them home in notes as family-time ideas for the preschoolers in your class.

87 Be Kind Suggestion Box

Keep a suggestion box for "Be Kind to Others" ideas near your dinner table or wherever your family has devotions. Jot down ideas for kind things that can be done for others and put them into the box. Once a week, let your child pick one suggestion from the box to do. Ideas might include calling a new neighbor, giving a family member a warm hug, or telling someone he or she looks nice.

88 God Made Food

When you shop with your preschooler, point out the many different kinds of fruits and vegetables in the store. If you are not in a rush, talk about where these foods came from. For example, apples grow on apple trees and God made trees.

Continue this conversation as your child helps you put away groceries or fix supper. Discuss how carrots, potatoes, and other fruits and vegetables, grew from tiny seeds in the ground. After each item is named, you and your child can say together, "And everything God made was good."

89 Learning to Share

Help your child learn to share by asking him or her to choose one or two books or toys in good condition to give to a child who doesn't have many. Or go shopping together and allow your child to buy two inexpensive toys or games; on the way home help your child place one in a drop box for a local charity.

90 Preparing for Church

Involve your child in preparations for church. Cleaning shoes, clearing out the car, laying out offering—all these chores can be done with the happy anticipation that "tomorrow is the day we worship God with our church family."

91 The Bible at Home

Let your child see that daily Bible reading is part of your family routine even though he or she cannot yet understand long Scripture passages. Try to schedule a time, perhaps before bedtime, when you can read simple Bible stories to your child and talk about what they mean.

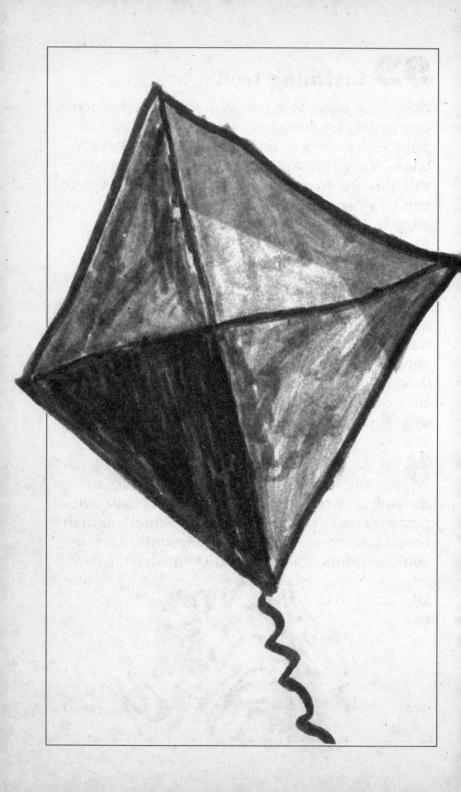

92 Giving to God

Help your child be a part of the giving experience by providing a container where your child can put coins for a Sunday school offering. A piggy bank, a pretty jar with a lid—almost anything will do. It might be fun to decorate a shoe box to use for offerings. Cut slots in the lid and add labels showing different ways your offerings are used.

93 I Can Help!

Assign your child specific chores to help at home. Keep a colorful chart with each day's chores checked off (brush teeth, put away toys, dust table) to encourage obedience in a fun way. Be sure to mention that we show love to God when we obey.

94 Our Family Rules

Draw simple pictures on paper listing your important family rules—"Don't hit brother"; "Wash hands before meals"; "Say please and thank you"; and so forth. Put the picture chart on the refrigerator to remind your child what he or she should do to be happy and make God happy, too.

95 Where Food Comes From

At a mealtime, name the different foods on the table that God has provided. Don't go into detail about where meat comes from. However, do talk about the sources of fruits, vegetables, bread, milk, and so on. As you name each food, thank God for it.

96 Family Christmas Program

Your whole family might want to have a Christmas program at home using robes and towels for costumes. You can take photographs and mount them in a notebook with the Christmas story. Then read it together during the holiday season.

97 Caring for Pets

Involve children in caring for family pets: feeding, watering, changing cage or litter, brushing, etc. Show children how to be gentle with animals and not startle them with loud noises or movements. Talk with preschoolers about the special way God made the cat's whiskers or soft hair. Tell children that God is pleased when we care for and enjoy the animals He has made.

98 Welcome to My House

Invite your pastor or child's Sunday school teacher for dessert. Encourage your child to participate in the preparations and in the conversation. Your child will have a new appreciation of the pastor or teacher as a real person.

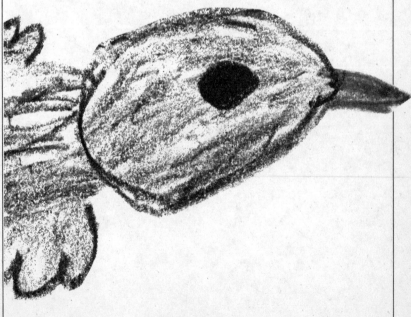

99 Pretend Restaurant

At lunch time, let children fix up a restaurant table and pretend they are being served or are serving in a restaurant. Take orders; bring the "special of the day" (soup, crackers, sandwich, and juice could be served). Remember good manners. Leave a tip!

100 Prayer Calendar

On a large calendar, write down the name of at least one person per day to remember with a special prayer. Keep it simple so that your child can understand and be a part of prayer time. During family devotional time or at your child's bedtime, talk about why you need to pray for that person. Then encourage your child to mention the person's name in prayer.